BRITAIN IN OLD

BISHOP'S STORTFORD
& SAWBRIDGEWORTH

WALLY WRIGHT

ALAN SUTTON PUBLISHING LIMITED

Alan Sutton Publishing Limited
Phoenix Mill · Far Thrupp · Stroud
Gloucestershire · GL5 2BU

First published 1995

Cover photographs: (front) Bridge Street, Bishop's Stortford, *c*. 1905; (back) Star Supply Stores, 46 Bell Street, Sawbridgeworth, late 1930s.

British Library Cataloguing in Publication Data.
A catalogue record for this book is available from the British Library.

ISBN 0–7509–0843–2

Typeset in 9/10 Sabon.
Typesetting and origination by
Alan Sutton Publishing Limited.
Printed in Great Britain by
Ebenezer Baylis, Worcester.

A decorative plaque on Sawbridgeworth Almshouses, commemorating Mr T.J. Mann, director of Mann, Crossman & Paulin brewers. His initials are incorporated into the design.

Contents

The Methodist church, South Street, Bishop's Stortford.

Introduction

Bishop's Stortford

The western edges of East Anglia largely consist of clay, gravel and sand. These are the residues of the melting ice sheets, and it was during the retreat of the last ice sheet some 10,000 years ago that melting outwash from the ice cut the valley of the River Stort, in which Bishop's Stortford is situated. Gravel from this process abounds in the area, and stone hand-axes of the first inhabitants have been found on the local gravel terraces.

Iron Age people from the continent of Europe were the first to establish themselves in the area. Tribes with the lyrical names of the Catuvellauni and the Trinovantes settled near the River Stort, and as part of their defences built the fort known as Wallbury Camp on the east bank of the river, south of the present town.

The Roman army invaded in AD 41 and later established a centre in Colchester. One of its first military roads, Stane Street (now the A120), ran westwards to Braughing, to give access to the East Midlands via Bishop's Stortford. To protect the river-crossing to the north of the town, a small fort was built and as happened elsewhere a separate local settlement became established near the fort. When disturbed by developers in 1953 the site of the settlement revealed many items, including a burial in a stone coffin, gold rings and domestic items of everyday use.

Edward, son of the Saxon king Alfred the Great, contained the Danish advance and settled a border along a line passing through the towns of Hertford, Bishop's Stortford and Witham, Essex. The remains of castles have been found at Hertford and Witham, but at Bishop's Stortford the remains are believed to be buried beneath the mound of Waytemore Castle, which dates from Norman times.

There may have been a castle at Bishop's Stortford from as early as 917, if the reference to 'Wigingamere' in 'The Anglo-Saxon Chronicle' is the same as the Norman 'Waytemore'. In the eleventh century the Normans recognized the military strength of the site and erected their motte and bailey earthwork on the foundations of the 'Saxon' castle. Surmounting the motte would have been the castle, originally built of wood, then of stone. The bailey extended to several acres, with many buildings within its walls, but the development of the town during the Middle Ages encroached on the castle precincts and all this has now gone.

At about the time of the Norman Conquest it is recorded that William, Bishop of London, purchased the manor of Bishop's Stortford, including the castle, from Edith the Fair, (King) Harold Godwin's lady. Bishop William died in 1075, and in the entry for Estarteford (Bishop's Stortford) in the 'Domesday Book' of 1086 the manor and castle were attributed to Bishop Maurice, Bishop of London; they had been granted to him that year by King William. The strong ecclesiastical connections developed by these holdings gave rise to the addition of 'Bishop's' to the town's name, and the holding of this land by the See of London survived for 600 years.

A prison was built adjacent to the castle. This was probably on the orders of the bishop, and was required by the Statute of Lambeth of 1261. The prison played its part in restraining malefactors, and records held in the Hertfordshire Record Office give detailed accounts for the years 1344–1474, including names of captives, survivors, costs and conditions. The normal fate of the inmates was to be chained to a wall or post, and it is perhaps not surprising that in 1292, of fifty-seven prisoners, twenty-nine died. In 1555 Bishop Edmund Bonner, under Queen Mary's influence, made great use of the prison but subsequently it was little used and was demolished in 1649.

During the Tudor and Stuart periods the town began to prosper, for it was then that its major industries of malting and leather tanning were established; these survived into the nineteenth century. The distinctive appearance of malthouses – long buildings with a pyramid kiln at one end – must have been a very common sight to the town's inhabitants. Some malthouses were near the river, as were the vats for leather tanning. These two processes gave rise to an effluvium; the former was like that of 'a well-baked fruit cake' but the latter was much more offensive. This, together with the smoke from the roasting of the barley, must have made a visit to the town on market day very memorable. The town was also known for its cordwainers (shoemakers) and leather workers, and one family was engaged in silk working.

Many buildings from the Jacobean era survive in the town, and a large proportion of them are public houses in a very good state of preservation. In many cases the timber beams of the framework have been exposed. Consequently it is possible to see how the centre of the town developed around the market square and the church. The public houses which most obviously date from early in Bishop's Stortford's history are the Black Lion, Half Moon and the Boar's Head. The White Horse is another fine example, though it is currently a restaurant.

The great interest of King Charles II and his Court in horse-racing brought many coaches from London to Newmarket. However, the roads were not metalled and could become treacherous. Consequently, instead of using the Great North Road through Ware, the alternative route, via Epping, was taken. To avoid the mêlée of Bishop's Stortford town centre the king had a bridge built in 1670 to cross the river at Southmill. This brought the traffic directly to the Hockerill crossroads, and, being halfway, it was a convenient overnight stopping-place. As a result this part of the town received much trade. To cater for the travellers four inns were established, one on each corner: the Red Lion, the Cock, the Coach and Horses, and the Crown, which became the most illustrious.

As a market town Bishop's Stortford has always been a focus for local trade and industry, and this has been very much associated with agriculture. To take advantage of the cereal growing that had been long established in East Anglia it was natural that malting should become the principal industry. To malt barley, the seed is first grown to convert the germ to maltose, an alternative form of sugar. When the sprout shows, heating stops the growth, but if the heating is continued it roasts the grains, and this imparts more colour and flavour to the brewed beer.

As a supplier of malt, Bishop's Stortford was not alone. It had strong competition from Hertford and Ware, which had the advantage of being able to transport goods by the navigable River Lee. In contrast the River Stort had too many shallows and meanders. Being inhibited in this way, Bishop's Stortford did not flourish until the river was made navigable in the eighteenth century. Production of malt reached its zenith in the first quarter of the nineteenth century.

In his diary Samuel Pepys records for 23 May 1688: '. . . and so away to Bishop's Stafford [sic]. The ways mighty full of water, so as hardly to be passed.' The bad road conditions imposed such a heavy cost on transporting the malt by packhorse from Bishop's Stortford to the brewers in London, that it made the business unprofitable. Sir George Jackson and Thomas Adderley, landlord of the Crown Inn, appreciated this problem, and co-founded the River Stort Navigation Company in 1766; the system opened in 1769. The company deepened and partially canalized the river, terminating the waterway with a basin at Bishop's Stortford that allowed barges to carry their cargo into the town. Close by was Wharf House, the country house of Sir George Jackson (later Sir George Duckett).

The effect of the navigation was to place the maltmakers on an equal footing with the competition, and the resulting increase in trade secured Bishop's Stortford's position as the hub of a wheel, along whose spokes flowed the barley from the farms in one direction, and the lime and manure – from London – in the other. With no serious competition from Essex, Bishop's Stortford, with its new bulk-transport facility, now enjoyed greater success than ever before, and at its peak the town had about forty malthouses, many of them small units with only two or three operators.

The euphoria of success was to receive a jolt when the effect of cheap grain from abroad, and quicker transport promised by the railway, were significant in diverting the barley away from Bishop's Stortford. By the end of the nineteenth century, malting had declined markedly, and today the town has no working malthouses.

The problem of road transport was eventually overcome by an enabling Act of Parliament (1696) for toll roads and turnpikes. In 1744 the Essex and Herts Highway Trust was formed to control the road from Harlow Common to Great Chesterford; the trustees included Sir Conyers Joscelyn of Hyde Hall, Isaac Whittington of Orford House, and William Sworder: all names with strong local connections. The statute required that certain conditions were met, with regard to weights carried and the width of the wheels, and the following table is an extract from a toll board of the renamed Hockerill Highway Trust for 1774:

Maximum loads	Summer		Winter	
	ton	cwt	ton	cwt
Waggon upon rollers [wheels] of the breadth of 16 in	8	0	7	0
Waggon with 6 in wheels	4	5	3	15
Cart with [2] wheels of breadth less than 6 in	1	10	1	7
Wheels less than 4.5 in	Not permitted			

Scale of charges

Coach with six horses	1s
Wain with three horses	3d
Horse laden or unladen	1d

Sir James McAdam was engineer to the Trust in 1822 and his improvements to road making enabled the turnpikes to remain profitable. However, despite local protestations in 1836, the railway reached Bishop's Stortford on 16 May 1842. The River Stort Navigation Company was also having difficulty in remaining solvent, and although its decline was slower than that of the turnpikes, the company was sold to Sir Walter Gilbey in 1898. Despite his great efforts, he gave up in 1905 after continued losses. The Lea Conservancy Board acquired the company in 1912, and in 1924 the first commercial boat was able to reach Bishop's Stortford again. The waterway is now used as a leisure facility for canoes, narrowboats and cruisers, under the care of British Waterways. In 1797 its engineeer said: 'the town of Bishop's Stortford is now open to the ports of the world.' It may still be true, but it does seem a little remote now.

People of fame, whether local or national, have been associated with the town through many centuries. Sir George Duckett is buried in St Michael's churchyard. As Sir George Jackson, he was a patron of Captain Cook and his memory is perpetuated in the names of Port Jackson, Australia, Jackson Bay, New Zealand, and, later, Jackson Square in Bishop's Stortford. He was also Secretary to the Treasury and was MP for Weymouth.

The monuments within St Michael's Church are not on a grandiose scale, but they do commemorate interesting people. One of the more illustrious is Lady Denny, wife of Sir Edward Denny; he was the son of Sir Anthony Denny, Privy Councillor to King Henry VIII. Lady Denny continued the Tudor connection as a maid of honour to Queen Elizabeth I.

Mention must be made here of Thomas Leigh. During the seventeenth century he spent forty-seven years as headmaster of the grammar school, which was attached to St Michael's churchyard. His school was described by an ex-pupil and famous local historian, Sir Henry Chauncy, as 'an excellent nursery that supplied both Universities with a great number of gentlemen who proved eminent in divinity, law and physic, and some in matters of State'. By the end of the century, however, the school had fallen into decline, the funds having been persistently misused by local dignitaries. Dr Thomas Tooke had to reinstitute it in 1690. The school library was nationally famous. When the school closed, following the death of Dr Tooke in 1721, the library was saved from dereliction by the Dimsdale family. Daniel Defoe said that 'the greatest ornament [of the town] is the school'. In 1767 Dr Samuel Johnson sent his negro servant, Francis Barber, to the school to learn Latin and Greek. The building was pulled down in 1768.

Probably the most famous gentleman to have been born in Bishop's Stortford was Cecil Rhodes, whose career and experiences in Oxford and South Africa are well documented. Not so well known is Revd F.W. Rhodes, Cecil's father and vicar of St Michael's Church. For twenty-six years he played a major part in furthering the education of the children of the town and he co-founded the Diocesan Training College for Schoolmistresses.

The Dimsdales were an outstanding Quaker family of Doctors of Medicine. In the seventeenth century there were three at one time practising in Hertford. Robert Dimsdale had settled in Bishop's Stortford on his return from escorting Will Penn to America in 1684. His grandson Thomas resided in Bishop's Stortford, and it was he who instigated inoculation against smallpox. After he had published a paper on his methods he was invited by the Empress Catherine of Russia to treat herself and her family. It is said that in the event of a mishap the precaution was taken of having a team of horses ready to carry him across and out of Russia. So successful was his visit that he was awarded many gifts and a Barony, still held by the family today.

The inns at Hockerill were patronized by many well-known travellers, some of whom visited the town centre. Samuel Pepys recorded in his diary some of his visits to Bishop's Stortford, and one entry states: 'Up betimes . . . and before night come to Bishop Stafford [sic], where Lowther and his friend did meet us again, and carried us to the Rayndeere [sic] Inn where Mrs Aynsworth, who lived hereforto at Cambridge, and whom I know better than they think for, do live. It was the woman, that, among other things, was great with my couzin Barnston, of Cottenham, and did used to sing to him, and did teach me – full forty times over – a very lewd song: a woman they are well acquainted with, and all the good fellows of the country come hither.' The husband, Edward Aynsworth, is immortalized in his issuing of a trade token inscribed with the word 'RAINDEARE'.

During the nineteenth century the town was fortunate in having local families of benefactors. Not only did they provide employment on the estates, they also made a positive contribution to the welfare of the community. The Gilbey brothers, Henry Parry and Walter (later Sir Walter), supported the Liberal Working Men's Club, and Sir Walter gave land to establish a hospital and a branch railway line. He also undertook the daunting task of trying to reinstate an ailing Navigation Company to bring back trade to Bishop's Stortford.

Mr Tresham Gilbey, son of Sir Walter, provided the ground for the cricket club. In 1929 his wife, Anne, daughter of Sir John Barker (founder of Barkers of Kensington), gave the town a swimming-pool in memory of her father.

As it has good road and rail connections Bishop's Stortford has had to suffer the pressures of progress. In 1966 a road improvement scheme threatened the demolition of the Corn Exchange, but the efforts of local societies gained a reprieve, and its conversion to offices and shops ensured its survival. In 1972 a major scheme for the middle of the town led to the removal of buildings, including Sir George Duckett's dwelling, Wharf House, to provide a multi-storey car-park and pedestrian shopping precinct. As the town follows the basic plan of a medieval settlement it did have serious car-parking problems.

The current pressures on Bishop's Stortford are again derived from transport: the development of Stansted Airport has led to a greater housing requirement. Since 1979 many new and extensive estates have been developed.

Bishop's Stortford is twinned with Villiers-sur-Marne, France, and Friedberg, Germany.

Sawbridgeworth

The name of Sawbridgeworth is very appropriate to a small town which spans two counties: its centre is in Hertfordshire but some of its estates are separated by the county border (River Stort) with Essex.

Recorded in the 'Domesday Book' as Sabrichtsworde, its name has been treated in a rather cavalier fashion over the centuries, and variations have included Sabbysford (1550), Sabysworth (1564), Sabsford (1635) and Sapsford (1900). The latter survives in the name of a local family. The railway station can claim to have the longest single name in the eastern region.

Considered in the eleventh century as the parish with the highest land value, it was effectively the capital of Braughing Hundred. Its value was more than double that of Bishop's Stortford – the reverse of the present situation.

The principal manors of Sayesbury and Pishiobury have a long and illustrious history. Beatrice de Saye was a third-generation descendant of King William I, and in 1189 she inherited the estate on the demise of her nephew, William de Mandeville, Earl of Essex. She passed it to her son, Geoffrey de Saye, and the manor was henceforth called Sayesbury. Pishiobury originated as a piece of land from the Sayesbury manor, granted to William FitzGerald in 1144. Some of its more notable owners were Lord Lisle (1337), John Chauncy (1400), Sir Walter Mildmay (1585) and Sir Thomas Hewyt (1600). The families of Chauncy, Mildmay and Hewyt all have fine monuments within the church. The manor was sold by Lord Scrope in 1534 to trustees, to be used by King Henry VIII, who granted it to Anne Boleyn.

With a watermill – mentioned in the 'Domesday Book' – and the nearby navigation, Sawbridgeworth was well served to supply malt, grain and flour to London.

Effectively, since the early nineteenth century Sawbridgeworth has been a quiet rural village. Although the increase in commuter residents has swelled the population to about 8,000, it still has many of these attributes.

Section One

SOUTH STREET

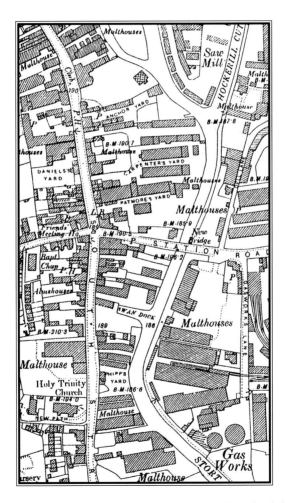

South Street is the southern arm of a cross formed by the principal roads of Bishop's Stortford. Being the main road between London and Cambridge, it was primarily used by coaches until the end of the seventeenth century, but with the opening of the navigation in 1769 South Street became the service road for the wharves and malthouses.

Looking towards Station Road, from near Holy Trinity Church, c. 1890. A cart is passing Phipp's yard, to the right of the picture, and the private house to the left is now the site of the Working Men's Club. Beyond is a large malthouse.

A closer view of the malthouse. The size of the building may be judged from the group of men standing by the entrance to the yard. The far end of the malting floors is visible to the left, and indicates the length of floor required to process a batch of malt by hand.

The fire at the Anchor Maltings on 2 December 1907. The fire started here and spread south before a brisk wind, to cross the navigation and threaten the gas works. Fire brigades were brought in from a wide area, and an eyewitness reported that the paint on the houses in Mount Pleasant 'ran down the doors'. The photograph was taken by Mr T. Bruxby of Bridge Street.

The scene of desolation after the fire. The report in the *Herts and Essex Observer* filled a whole page.

Looking towards Station Road, *c.* 1890. The gentleman on the right stands by the entrance to a malthouse yard, and in the left foreground is the entrance to Anchor Yard, which had a loading wharf on the navigation. The Anchor Inn, at no. 23, is first mentioned in 1680 and survived until 1963. It is now the site of Sainsbury's supermarket.

A picture taken from the same position as above, 1915. On the west side (right) of the street a considerable degree of change has taken place; brick buildings have replaced the wooden structures. On the right is the Albert temperance hotel; next to it is the post office, and then the Methodist church, built in 1903. The Army is much in evidence – the men are probably collecting the fodder ration from Cowell's store.

Skelton's warehouse had a false front and parapet added, as required by the prevailing fashion of the eighteenth century, but the steep roof suggests that a seventeenth-century timber structure remained inside. The building near the corner of the road, with railings and an advertisement board, is the Liberal Working Men's Club. The photograph dates from about 1890.

Compared with the view above only the turn in the road and the projecting building had remained unaltered by about 1950. A marked increase in vehicles is the most obvious difference. Here, an ambulance is coming out of its station.

Daisy Day FRPS, who achieved great renown as a portrait photographer in the 1920s. These are two of her studies. She was the one of the first women to achieve the much coveted Fellowship of the Royal Photographic Society.

Joseph Dorrington Day, Daisy's father, was a stonemason, builder and brickmaker. His house and yard at 100 South Street were adjacent to the malthouse and included the photographic studio. Mr Day was a strong temperance man and regularly arranged the children's Sunday school outings.

The Fire Station frontage of 22 South Street shows the date 1898. Also in evidence are the changes that were made to widen the entrance, to accommodate both the fire and ambulance vehicles. Space here was very limited and it closed in 1970.

The Liberal Working Men's Club commenced in 1873, and thanks to the generosity of Mr Henry Parry Gilbey it soon moved to 16 South Street, which had an adjacent single-storey reading room. The club was a great boon to the temperance movement and to the social life of the townsfolk, and, with few changes, it remained consistently successful. The club acquired its present site next to Holy Trinity Church in 1937. To the left of the photograph, the decorated façade belongs to the Empire Picture Palace.

A performance of *The Gondoliers* by the Bishop's Stortford Amateur Operatic Society, 1931. This was one of the many functions held at the Great Hall. The old Agricultural Hall from Kilburn was acquired at the instigation of Henry Parry Gilbey, the president of the Liberal Working Men's Club, and installed in the club's grounds in 1879, as a lecture and entertainment centre for its members.

Henry Parry Gilbey, elder brother of Walter, was born at The Links, Windhill. He greatly assisted the founding of the Liberal Working Men's Club in 1874. When he died in 1892, the whole of Bishop's Stortford closed down for the occasion of his funeral.

18

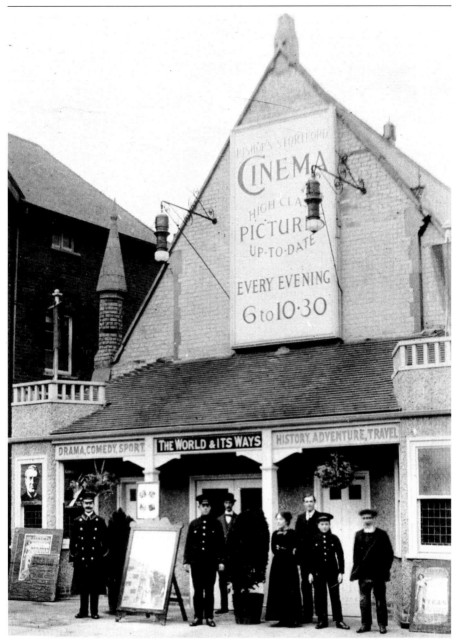

No. 1 South Street. This building started life as a Wesleyan chapel (see p. 20). It was converted into a cinema in 1911. In 1916 it was purchased by Mr E.E. Smith, who modified the cinema and reopened it in 1919. It flourished throughout the '20s. The first talkie to be screened there, in February 1931, was *Love Parade* with Maurice Chevalier. The cinema, now 'old-fashioned', was closed in May 1932.

The Wesleyan chapel, *c.* 1900. This opened in 1866 and closed in 1903, except for Pleasant Sunday Afternoons temperance meetings. In 1911 the chapel was converted into a cinema. It opened, with admission by invitation only, on 10 February 1912. Mr Hatrick was the manager.

With the closure of the cinema (see p. 19), and the Regent firmly established, Mr E.E. Smith renovated the old cinema. He increased the seating capacity to 500, including some 'cosy' double seats. It was renamed the Phoenix and showed mostly popular repeat and H (Horror) certificate films. A particular success in 1948 was *For Whom the Bell Tolls*, which ran for a week.

A 'for sale' board signifies the demise of the Granada (formerly the Regent). Film shows by the Smith family had run for fifty-five years. Stevens' shops, next to the cinema, were owned by Percy and Wilfred Stevens, who ran the radio and music shops respectively.

Percy's window display in 1928, when 78 r.p.m. records and wireless sets were the leading products. There were no TVs or 'trannies'. The sunrise fretwork adorns a 1927 PYE four-valve, portable battery receiver with internal aerial.

The Regent

BISHOP'S STORTFORD

Sole Proprietor .... ERNEST E. SMITH
Manager .... G. P. A. SMITH

PROGRAMME FOR
APRIL 1933

NIGHTLY 6 to 10.30   (Sat. from 5.45)
MATINEES, THURSDAY and SATURDAY at 2.30
Phone 456   FREE CAR PARK

With seating for 999 people this was the cinema for the talkies. Designed by Mr E.M. Allen-Hallett and built by F. Cannon & Son, it was opened by Rear Admiral Murray-Sueter on 9 November 1931.

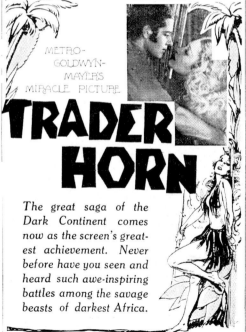

METRO-GOLDWYN-MAYER'S
MIRACLE PICTURE

TRADER HORN

The great saga of the Dark Continent comes now as the screen's greatest achievement. Never before have you seen and heard such awe-inspiring battles among the savage beasts of darkest Africa.

To celebrate the opening, a reception was held at the Railway Hotel. A souvenir programme was issued and the film *Trader Horn*, starring Harry Carey, was screened.

Mr Arthur Maxwell, at 27 Potter Street, was a well-known photographer in Bishop's Stortford. His shop, opposite Church Street, was next door to the Methodist chapel (formerly the Wesleyan chapel). In the far distance is the double-gabled house of the Misses Nash. The photograph dates from about 1900.

Church Street. The old building in the centre left, seen here enclosed by later development, was typical of the Tudor timber-framed buildings in Bishop's Stortford. Most have now been hidden or replaced. This building, now demolished, would have been on the southernmost edge of the medieval town.

St Michael's (C. of E.) Infants' School and soup kitchen. Built in about 1880, it combined the services of supplying the poor with hot soup for 1*d* per quart in the winter with schooling for 150 children.

Pupils of St Michael's Junior School display the national dress of many countries, to celebrate Empire Day, *c.* 1932. Back row, left to right: Joyce Clarke, Doris Sampford, -?-, Eileen Hinkston, -?-, Middle row: Daphne Smith, Leonard King, Joyce Zelley, Joyce Swan, -?-, Betty Sadler. Front row: Neil Watts, Pat Trew, -?-.

The Technical Institute, at 3 Church Street, was built in about 1891. In about 1910 the headmaster for art was Mr Leonard Lacy, while the technical headmaster was Mr Richard Bunn. With these two divisions the institute could cater for many requirements. It closed in about 1970.

The woodwork class had a variety of machines. Putting them to good use are, left to right: Stan Coxall, Arthur Wyatt, Wally Wright (not the author), Reg Pannell. The photograph dates from about 1923.

The Volunteer Fire Brigade display their extending ladder outside their station in South Street, *c.* 1918. Standing to the left is Lieutenant F. Glasscock. To the right is Captain A.S. Barrett.

POTTER STREET,
MARKET SQUARE

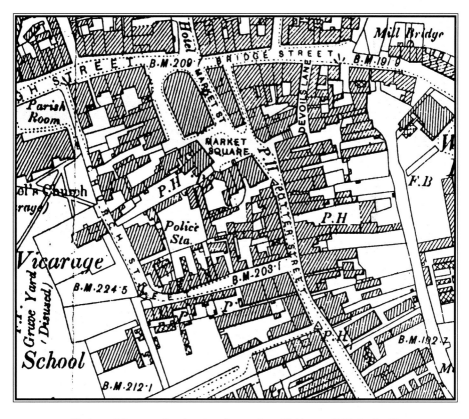

The heart of the town, where throughout the centuries stallholders would fill the air with

their cries as they proclaimed their best bargains. Areas known as Shop Row, Fish Row,

Leather Market and Poultry Hill indicate the products which were available here on Tudor

market days.

In 1890 Benjamin Nind Beard was trading as a draper in no. 9 (later known as Waterloo House). Henry Laugher, an outfitter, was next door, and nearest the camera is Thomas Lee's ironmongery.

The premises of Robert Lock, after the fire of about 1900. Lock advertised as a draper, shawlman and Manchester warehouseman; he claimed to stock the best cotton products. Pictured from left to right are: ? Osborne, George Thickings (dairyman), a policeman, Captain A. Slaps Barrett, Lt F. Glasscock, Fred Nash (maltster), Bert Willcocks, J. Millard (fireman), Tom Radley. Robert Lock's was the predecessor to Scarfe's.

Crowds line the street during a visit by the Prince of Wales. In the background are Waterloo House and the three shops that Sir Walter Gilbey had built on the site of Thomas Lee's store. In between is the grocery shop, Bon Marché. On the corner to the right is the Plume of Feathers public house, mentioned in records of 1681 as 'Ed Ashby's house at ye ffeathers in ye Leather Market'.

A MERRY CHRISTMAS

The same location, on a different occasion. It is possibly Edward VII's coronation – notice the soldiers. The card was printed in Germany.

Except for the ground-floor windows this frontage is typical of the seventeenth century. The photograph dates from about 1878, and at that time the building was occupied by Mr Geo. Sapsford, butcher and slaughterer. Later it was restored, and it is now Clement Joscelyne's.

The Curriers Arms, *c.* 1880. Mr F. Clarke stands in the doorway. The inn was named after the skin-dressing trade which had been established in this area. In 1830 the landlord, Mr James Franklin, was tried for the murder of his wife but was acquitted for lack of evidence. The inn closed in 1905. The small shop on the right sold antiques.

An engraving of the Kings Head by C.L. Tyler, dated 1828. The building was demolished in 1826 to make way for the Corn Exchange. It had operated as a tavern (selling wine) for 150 years; hence its sign shows a bunch of grapes.

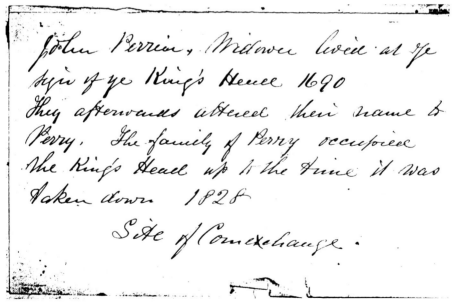

Text taken from the back of the above. It states that John Perrin, widower, lived at the pub in 1690. The family changed their name to Perry. They continued to occupy the pub until its demolition.

The Corn Exchange was designed by Mr Lewis Vuilliamy and built in 1828. This sketch shows the original ornamentation on the Corn Exchange which included a statue of Ceres over the entrance. Ceres was the Roman goddess of the earth and especially of grain.

North Street, looking towards the Corn Exchange, *c.* 1890. Its embellishments have been removed and the glass cover installed. The porch to the right of the photograph is the entrance to the Urban District Council offices, and in the distance is Market Square.

The trading area of the Corn Exchange, where the sixty-five dealers each had a desk. The glass roof is prominent. It admitted the daylight required to judge the quality of the grain, and provided dry conditions not previously enjoyed.

The rear of the Corn Exchange, *c.* 1905. Mr E.E. Smith's hairdressing salon is on the corner, behind the group of men, and Mr F. Smith's salon is to the rear of Market Square.

The original Reindeer Inn of Samuel Pepys fame, on the corner with the High Street. It traded from about 1644 to 1810. Part of the roof of an earlier building shows behind the façade. In 1666 the landlord Edward Ainsworth issued two tokens. These were given to customers as small change and could be used locally as coinage. One is shown below. His wife Betty was renowned for her 'hospitality' and is twice mentioned in Pepys' diary.

The token issued by Edward Ainsworth. It has a reindeer motif. There were many different types of tokens in circulation in the seventeenth century to overcome the shortage of small change.

NORTH STREET

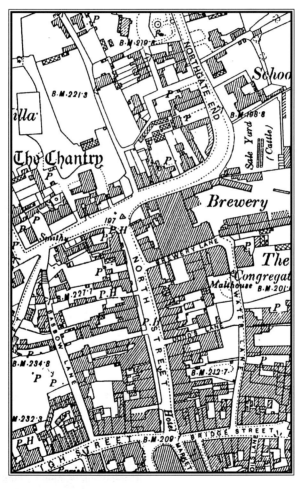

North Street has been fronted with fine buildings since its

earliest development, and for many years it has served as the 'best end'

of town, catering for the people with more expensive tastes.

The George is the oldest recorded inn in Bishop's Stortford – records of it date from 1417. In 1629 it was graced by King Charles I, who 'dyned at ye George' to the ringing of the church bells. The Manor of Piggotts held its court here during the fifteenth century, and favoured the Hawkins family. By 1700 the Hawkinses had held the property for 300 years. It is not perhaps surprising that there have been reports of ghostly manifestations in some rooms after so long a history.

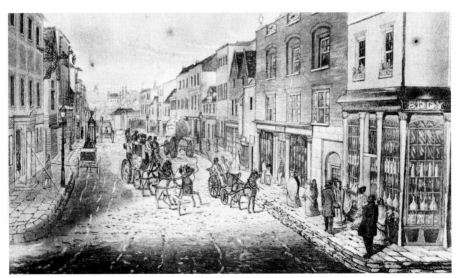

The view from the Corn Exchange, *c.* 1842. This sketch shows the recently installed gas lighting, and many of the shops on the right are easily recognizable today. In the distance is Lindsell's windmill on Barrells Down.

Parades at Easter and Whitsun were a regular occurrence, but royal celebrations like this were extra special. This is Queen Victoria's jubilee of 'sixty glorious years' and much attention has been lavished on all the decorations. Mr Barrett's shop on the right shows his flair for rich displays.

The vantage point of the Corn Exchange was a cameraman's gift and this photograph has captured the onset of the motor car, *c.* 1918. However, the two tall policemen could easily maintain an atmosphere of law and order. The registration number, LA4243, of the car second from left was issued in 1910.

An active Thursday market, 1950. No record exists of the granting of the right to hold a market in the town. However, the market is referred to in an account of 1431 which cites Potters (Market) Cross. Many of the street signs will be familiar to present-day shoppers, but the road sign indicating that London is to the north might be a hangover from the days when it was felt necessary to confuse the enemy.

The market in 1971, with plenty of fruit and clothing, and a discussion between a lady and the stall-holder.

Alfred Slaps Barrett entered into partnership with Mr Holland in 1890. Their grocery shop at 18 North Street, with its fancy cast-iron window frames, is shown here displaying a Bovril sticker. Full aprons were the order of the day for shop serving staff.

Shown here to the right is Mr Harry Mardon's printing works, which produced the *Herts and Essex Observer* for seventy-three years until 1961. The decorated window, no. 14, is that of Speechly & Milbank, the chemists, whose capitals were carved by Italian workmen on the pavement at the time of its restoration in about 1880. Holland & Barrett's shop has a white frontage and it carries the figure of a hart mounted on its facia. The hart was the emblem of the 1st Herts Light Horse Regiment and originally surmounted the Silver Leys barracks. On the regiment's disbandment Mr Holland acquired the piece and placed it here. The hart has recently been renovated and is shown here (inset) on no. 14.

The interior of Speechly & Milbank's chemist shop at 14 North Street, showing the rows and rows of basic materials ready to be made up into prescriptions.

On the left is Mr Sydney Milbank. In about 1900 the lids of cream pots were used as an advertising device. Those with a black and white design were in common use, though many chemists took advantage of colour painted scenes. These items are now sought after by collectors of ceramics.

The Chequers, at no. 19. This coaching inn and posting house was first recorded in 1684. It played an active part in providing accommodation and stabling in the town until it closed in 1950. The advertisement in H. Copley's *Advertiser and Record* of 1888 stated that the Chequers omnibus attended at the station for the arrival and departure of every train.

The well-known landlord of the Chequers and a town councillor was Joseph Brazier, a popular and jocular man. He was the subject of a painting by Mr John Kirkby, which was hung in the Royal Academy.

Dr Robert Wallace, an Australian, lived and practised in no. 27, shown here on the left. A straightforward surgeon, he used to attend to any minor operations at his patients' home, while regaling them with stories of his guns and shooting forays after the local rats. The adjacent building is the White Horse. It is finished in the East Anglian style with pargetting, which uses a low relief design impressed into the wet mortar. The interior contains some fine moulded woodwork and may date from about 1500.

Sir Walter Gilbey, Bart. As a young man he courted Ellen Parish, daughter of the landlord of the White Horse. They married in 1858 and subsequently lived at Elsenham Hall. They had nine children.

Fowler's, 20 North Street. The shop provided a service to the town for over forty years. It is shown here dressed for Christmas with poultry, rabbits, pheasants and sides of beef and pork, ready for delivery to its customers.

King Edward VII's car passing through Bishop's Stortford, 31 October 1905. The fire brigade had erected a celebratory arch outside the Council offices in North Street.

The band of the Volunteer Rifle Corps assembled on parade in North Street, 1868. This band became the first company band of the 1st Herts Volunteer Regiment.

The brewery in Water Lane. The brewery was built in 1780 by the Hawkeses, a Bishop's Stortford family of brewers long established in Herts. The brewery and 157 pubs were acquired by Benskins in 1898 and the brewery was closed in 1916. The site was used as a depot by Ind Coope until developed as a supermarket in 1994.

The wedding of Alexandra and Edward, Prince of Wales, 1863. This is one of the earliest surviving photographs of Bishop's Stortford, and shows one of the seven truly sumptuous arches of evergreens erected for the occasion. The house to the right is a private residence. On the opposite corner is the Half Moon, another of the seventeenth-century buildings in the town. The landlord, one Zachariah Colls, came to the town a poor man, and as a journeyman farrier he progressed to horse-dealer and publican.

The same location in 1890. By this time the Half Moon has become a Hawkes public house, and the house opposite is now Amos Pryor's shop. Gas lighting has reached this end of the town, and the Chantry buildings beyond have been altered.

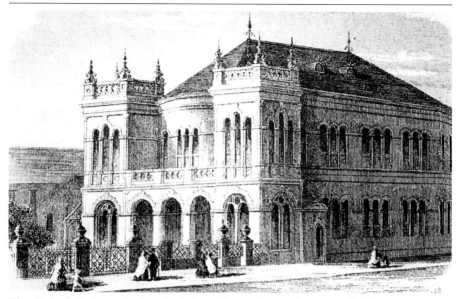

The United Reformed church, Water Lane. From the Act of Toleration 1689, Nonconformists received a limited freedom to worship. Samuel Cradock was an early minister, in 1700, but conversions were slow. The present church, consecrated in 1869, was designed by W.H. Poulton and built in the Italianate style. It has a wealth of decorative cast-ironwork and several memorials within, one of which is to Alfred Slaps Barrett.

General Booth, founder of the Salvation Army, travelled widely to give his sermons and he visited Bishop's Stortford on 16 July 1907. Here an elderly lady is strongly making her point, which the general appears to be carefully considering.

NORTHGATE END, RYE STREET

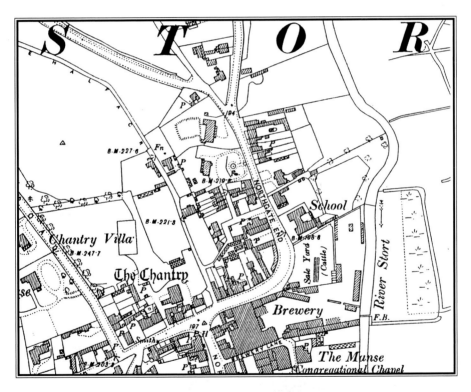

The name of The Chantry, in Hadham Road, suggests the close association this area had

with the early Church. Northgate clearly derives from the medieval entrance to the town,

but the exact location of the gate is not recorded; most likely it was at the junction of North

Street and Hadham Road. Above, Rye Street is the right fork of Northgate End.

Cattle Market. Messrs Sworders modernized the market in 1929; further alterations were made in 1969 and again in 1982. The 100th Christmas Fat Stock Show was held in 1972 and the last sale was in December 1982.

The last beast sold at the last sale, under the hammer of Mr A.V. Muskett of Sworders.

Dr Charles Hodson, with some of his family and staff, in front of The Chantry, *c*. 1865. Dr Hodson made all the visits to his patients on horseback, and covered a very wide area.

The Northgate British School received its first Treasury grant of £150 in 1840, though it was mainly supported by the Congregational Church. It was later known as the Northgate Primary School and moved to new premises in Cricketfield Lane in 1968.

DAY	CLASS	S.55 9.G.C.			9.55	10	10.45		11	11.45
MONDAY	1. 3. 2. 4. 5.				Religious Instruction	1. Arith. 3. Arith. 2. Arith. 4. Arith. 5. Arith.			1. Gram. 3. Read. 2. Geog. 4. Read. 5. Read.	1. V 3. C 2. F 4. C 5. C
TUESDAY	1. 3. 2. 4. 5.				Religious Instruction	1. Arith. 3. Arith. 2. Arith. 4. Arith. 5. Arith.			1. Geog. 3. Writ. 2 Gram. 4. Read. 5 Geog.	1. F 3. C 2. F 4. V 5. F
WEDNESDAY	1. 3. 2. 4. 5.				Religious Instruction	1. Arith. 3. Arith. 2. Geog. 4. Writ. 5. Object			1. Science 3. Writ. 2. Science 4. Geog 5. Arith.	1. F 3. C 2. A 4. F 5 F
THURSDAY	1. 3. 2. 4. 5.				Religious Instruction	1. Geog. 3. Writ. 2. Arith. 4. Arith. 5. Arith.			1. Writ. 3. Read. 2. Gram. 4. Writ. 5. Gram.	1. F 3. C 2. V 4. C 5. F
FRIDAY	1. 3. 2. 4. 5.				Religious Instruction	1. Gram. 3. Arith. 2. Arith. 4. Geog. 5. Arith.			1. Arith. 3. Read. 2. Writ. 4. Arith. 5. Geog.	1. V 3. C 2. 4. F 5. F

Vertical columns: Assembling. · Prayers. (before 9.55); Rotters / Recreation (between 10.45 and 11)

Recreation on Friday Afternoons to the Class

The non-sectarian British School placed a very strong emphasis on the three Rs. The inspector's report on general standards could influence the size of the grant for the following year. This one is dated 23 April 1894. All groups had a lesson in music and

	12-2.10	3.	3.10 3.45	4.15	
Grace and Dismissal · Assembling · Registers		1.\ 3 2.} Draw. 4. 5.	1. Read. 3. Writ. 2. Writ. 4. Geog. 5. Tables	1. Maps 3. Music 2. Arith. 4. Music 5. Writ.	Prayers and Dismissal
		1. Poetry 3. Word. Bd. 2. Read. 4. Word. Bᵈ 5. Music	1. C. Bks. 3. Poetry 2. C. Bks. 4. Poetry 5. Read.	1. Music 3. Read. 2. Music 4. Writ. 5. Writ.	
Recreation	1.\ 3. 2.} Draw 4. 5.		1. Writ. 3. Gram. 2. Poetry 4. Writ. 5. Writ.	1. Word Bˢ 3. Read. 2. Writ. 4. Arith. 5. Tables &c	Dismissal
		1. Arith. 3. Arith. 2. Writ. 4. Read. 5. Poetry	1. Citizensh 3. Writ. 2. Maps or} 4. Tables } 5. Drill	1. Writ. 3. Read. 2. Read. 4. Writ. 5. Read.	
		1.\ 3. 2.} Draw. 4. 5.	1. Spelling 2. Do. 3. Obj. Les. ʳʳ writ. 4. Do. 5. Music	1. Music 3. Do. 2. Do. 4. Do. 5. Writ.	

ch makes the best attendance each week, 3.10- 3.45.

some in citizenship, but group 4 had double writing on three days and two music lessons to make up for it.

A procession to celebrate the coronation of King George VI, 22 June 1911. The crowd has spilled into Hadham Road. Note the fashions of the period.

The Eagle. Formerly Mr Cannon's bakery, it was used as a public house and general shop from 1865 to 1896, when the building was demolished.

Rye Street Hospital. This was built in memory of Mr Bartle J.L. Frere of Twyford House, Thorley, to a design by Mr Eustace C. Frere FRIBA. The capital for the hospital was raised by his widow and their children and also by public subscription. Sir Walter Gilbey gave the land.

The Duchess of York (Elizabeth, the Queen Mother) arriving to open a new wing at Rye Street Hospital, 18 May 1933.

Accompanied by Mr Tresham Gilbey, the duchess was received at the hospital by Viscount Hampden, Lord Lieutenant of Hertfordshire.

Here, the cottage hospital is to the left and very close to the Fox public house, on the other side of the road. In the distance is a building which was the Plough public house from 1861 until 1923, when it became a private residence.

The Fox. There were two public houses by this name, the other being in South Street. This was very small. It closed in 1993, and the site was developed as a housing estate.

WINDHILL, HIGH STREET, BRIDGE STREET

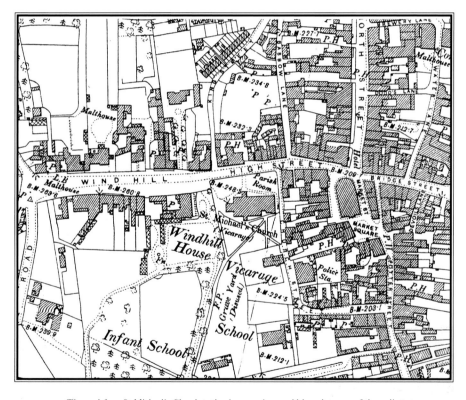

The road from St Michael's Church to the river crossing would have been one of the earliest

to be lined with shops and houses, to lodge and sustain the traveller during his overnight

stay. Before it was shortened High Street included Bridge Street and extended as far as the

Causeway.

Windhill was developed in the eighteenth and nineteenth centuries, and was where the wealthy, professional people lived. In 1818 Henry Gilbey moved to The Links, seen here to the right, by the group of people. The wideness of the road recalls the fairs that were held three times a year to raise money for the church. The profits of many 'May ales' are recorded in the churchwardens' accounts; the 'May ale' of 1515 grossed 50s.

Henry Gilbey. Five of his nine children were born at The Links, including Henry Parry, Walter and Alfred. In 1823 Henry started a daily coach service to Cambridge and later to the Bull in the Aldwych, London. However, the Northern and Eastern Railway Company brought the railway to Bishop's Stortford in 1842. The prospect of this competition had led Henry Gilbey to move to the Red Lion, Hockerill, in 1841. However, he died in 1842.

Set upon high ground, well above the flood plain, St Michael's is believed to be of Saxon foundation. A road runs direct from it to the crossing of the River Stort and what was once a marsh area. The present church was built in the fifteenth century, in the local style with flint facings. The tower was raised and a spire added at the end of the eighteenth century; together they are 182 ft high. Henry Gilbey is buried in the churchyard and within the church are memorials to the founders of the navigation, Sir George Duckett and Thomas Adderly. There is also a memorial to Lady Margaret Denny, maid of honour to Queen Elizabeth I.

One of the eighteen misericords in St Michael's Church. These date from the early fifteenth century and are believed to have come from Old St Paul's, London. This one portrays a lady in a hood.

Tissiman's at 11 and 13 High Street. These two buildings are the oldest known timber-framed structures in Bishop's Stortford. In no. 11 is a Wealden-type framework that may date from about 1450, and no. 13 contains some early construction and attractively worked carvings of acanthus leaves.

Bridge Street, with the Black Lion in the foreground, *c.* 1890. Apart from the distant brick building, the scene is almost exactly as it would have been in about 1650.

An Easter parade, *c.* 1910. Here, the Black Lion has been completely renovated by Mr J.L. Glasscock, and with the plaster removed and the windows exposed, it is very close to its original appearance of about 1600. The boy to the left is John Knight; he was on his way home, having bought a pennyworth of gunpowder for his mother to clean the chimney.

The view eastwards, with the Black Lion on the right, *c.* 1905. The first building on the left is the Star tavern, no. 7, whose existence was first recorded in 1616. At the time of this photograph the landlord was Mr L. Kilroy. Further along were the premises of Mr F. Handscomb, who retailed agricultural hand tools, and Mr F. Chaplin, who made horse collars. The McMullen house is the Cat and Fiddle, which closed in 1909. The proprietor was Miss Philpott. On the right is Waterman's tobacco and music shop, and next door is Brangham's, the fruiterer and florist.

In this snowy scene is the Shades public house, unusual in having a name unknown elsewhere in Hertfordshire or Essex. The disc on the end wall declares a 10 mph speed limit, and the railings on the right mark the millrace and the entrance to Flynn's malthouse yard.

The Town Mill. The millrace passed under the road to drive the waterwheel. The mill, first mentioned in the 'Domesday Book', ceased working in 1890. It was pulled down and the site was later developed as a shopping precinct, in 1973. To the left of the mill is the Shades, and on the extreme right, and below, is Mr Christy's shop.

Christy's whitesmith's shop. Joseph Christy was a tinsmith and brazier at this shop from 1854. His son Charles Clarence Christy took over in 1894 at the age of thirty-seven.

The millrace, looking north from Bridge Street, *c.* 1950. The house survives virtually unaltered, but the kiln tops of the malthouse in Flynn's yard have now gone.

A sketch of Flynn's maltings by Mr H.P. King, 1951.

THE CAUSEWAY, HOCKERILL

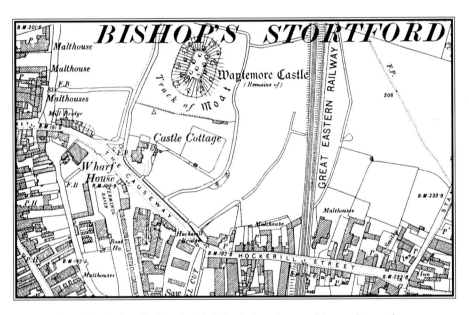

The castle and prison played a major role during the formative years of the town, but now they are reduced to a mound and public park for the benefit of the town's residents. Hockerill crossroads vied with the town centre in providing board and lodging for the coach travellers on the road to Newmarket, and although it is still a busy junction for today's motor cars, the passengers seldom tarry for more than a few minutes.

A sketch portraying Waytemore Castle as it might have been in the twelfth century.

The Norman motte of the castle is in very good condition and clearly demonstrates the scale and shape of the earthwork. King John demolished Waytemore Castle during a religious dispute but was made to rebuild it, and spent a night in the new structure in 1216 to prove its worth. Some remains of this rebuilt castle may still be seen.

Adjacent to the castle a prison was built. Although the castle was abandoned by the fifteenth century the prison continued to do duty until 1649, when it was demolished during the Commonwealth. One prisoner during Elizabethan times was Sir Thomas Pound, a member of the Catholic Society of Jesus. He is shown here being manacled. Pound suffered some thirty years in various gaols for his beliefs.

The entrance to the open-air swimming-pool. This was presented to the town in 1924 by Mrs Tresham Gilbey, in memory of her father, Sir John Barker. It closed in 1973 to become part of the new shopping precinct.

Hughes timber-yard and foundry. On the left is the shop which made moulds for the many products cast in brass and iron. The company made various domestic items and specialized in school desks. Latterly the yard was used by J.L. Glasscock's, the builder.

The Black Bull was on the corner of Dane Street and Hockerill Street and may have replaced the Bull, a disorderly house closed down in 1569. Jack Aycliffe was the landlord when the Black Bull closed in 1920. The mansard roof to the left survived when the corner site was developed in the more impressive neo-Georgian style.

The United Match Industries factory. Match production was started in the town by E.H. King & Company in 1923. In 1928 the business became United Match Industries. In 1929 it built this well-known local landmark. The business provided employment for many local people, until it went into voluntary liquidation in 1970 owing to a reduction in demand and competition from cheaper, imported matches. The factory was demolished in about 1974. The inset shows one of the labels.

The start of a million or more matches. A First World War lorry loaded with chemicals is parked beside a stack of logs, *c.* 1929.

Crown Inn. This very extensive and well-appointed inn dated from the sixteenth century and had a clientele that included Daniel Defoe, the Prince Regent and Princess Victoria. The site included a malthouse and brewery. In the 1890s it became a boys' school, and was demolished in 1898. Visible on the extreme left is part of the malthouse.

The Crown malthouse and brewery, looking towards the 'dangerous crossroads', according to the sign. On the end wall of the malthouse is the emblem of the Crown and part of the name W.R. Percival, who was the landlord from 1827 to 1834. He was the last to run it as a posting inn.

Hockerill crossroads was a very busy intersection between the Colchester–Braughing and the London–Newmarket roads. It was brought into eminence when King Charles II built Southmill bridge to create a bypass to the town. Each corner had an inn for the benefit of travellers, and this sketch of 1850 by C.C. Harper shows the Cock Tavern and the Red Lion. Henry Gilbey moved to the Red Lion in 1841.

The Coach & Horses was the last of the four crossroads inns to be built. In 1771 it was owned by Richard Thompson who was also a postmaster. A servant, Ann Cannon, was charged in 1795 with stealing a letter containing money and was sentenced to be hanged, though ultimately she was acquitted. The house lost its postal licence as a result but continued to trade until 1980, when it closed and was converted into offices.

George Thickings, dairyman of Castle Street, who took his herd twice a day to the fields by All Saints' Church, *c.* 1930. The fountain was raised in memory of Brigadier Eyre, alias Mr George Bramston Archer-Houblon of Great Hallingbury. It is now sited in the Castle Gardens.

In 1824 Henry Gilbey's coach made regular daily journeys to London, and travelling outside in winter must have been an arduous experience. Fares were 4s outside, 8s inside.

HADHAM ROAD, DUNMOW ROAD

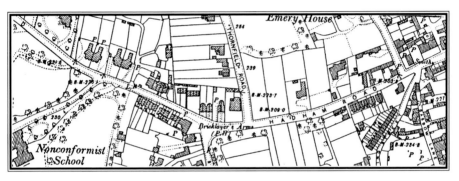

Hadham Road (above) and Dunmow Road (below) follow very closely the line of the Roman Stane Street from Colchester to Braughing. These roads cross the outskirts of town, where the pesthouse and workhouse would have been found. Today's needs are for light industrial parks and supermarkets.

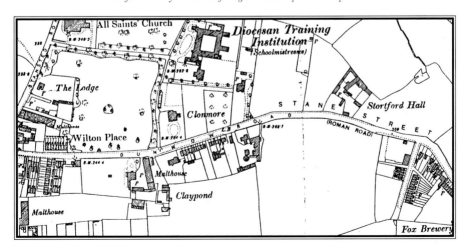

Bishop's Stortford Collegiate School. Following the initiative of John Wesley in 1764 an independent school was started in Bishop's Stortford. It moved to its present site in 1852 and was known as the Nonconformist Grammar School until 1901, when it adopted its present title of Bishop's Stortford College. Today it is a well-known independent public school, and students have been received mainly from the trade and professional classes.

The grammar school. This fine building was set up by Revd F.W. Rhodes in about 1855. Thus continued the provision of education in Bishop's Stortford, which had been virtually unbroken since the bequest of £5 per annum by Margaret Dane in 1579. The school was strongly Anglican. After a chequered history, it was closed in 1930 and demolished in 1978.

Rayment's Forge. Sid and Arthur Rayment ran the last shoeing smithy in Bishop's Stortford until it closed in 1970.

Sid Rayment rolls up a tyre for a wheel. After joining up the ends he would reheat the tyre and allow it to shrink on to, and firmly hold together, the rim of the wooden wheel.

The St Albans Diocesan Training College for Schoolmistresses was opened in 1852. A Provisional Committee purchased 2½ acres of land and the college was built to the design of Mr Joseph Clarke. The bricks were made from the local clay and burnt on site. The school suffered some damage during the Second World War and finally closed in 1979, under a governmental cost-saving scheme.

Revd J. Menet, vicar of All Saints' Church, who was the chaplain and principal of the college.

The fire that destroyed All Saints' Church on 21 June 1935. The church was designed and built in 1851 by Mr G.E. Pritchett, to serve one of the three new parishes formed when the old parish was divided up by Revd F.W. Rhodes.

This sketch shows the building in its original form. After the fire a new church, designed by Mr S. Dykes-Bower, was consecrated by the Bishop of St Albans on 25 July 1937.

A public house with sporting connections. It was converted from a farmhouse owned by the footballer Mr Ted Sylvester, who was born there. The pub was later owned by Mr L. Larman of local cricketing fame. In 1934 it was replaced by the present building, to continue the supply of refreshments to people on the new estates.

The Union Workhouse. Each parish had its own workhouse to care for the poor, until the 1834 Poor Law Amendment Act required that the poor of twenty-one local parishes in Herts and Essex transfer their claimants to Bishop's Stortford. The Board of Guardians was replaced by Herts County Council in 1930, and the site became the Herts and Essex Hospital, following its use as a wartime emergency unit.

Mrs Ellen Friend and nurses pose by an entrance to the old workhouse, 1935. Mrs Friend was a matron for twenty-seven years.

Mr and Mrs Holland, both porters, are seen here in fancy dress, ready for a party. Their daughter Patricia is wearing the pointed hat, and Matron's daughter Phyllis is in the butterfly costume.

Christmas day in the workhouse. Matron pulls a cracker with the senior nurse as they wait to welcome the inmates to a special treat.

The windmill, Dunmow Road. This was built in 1766, and was situated close to the Fox brewery and Union Workhouse. This was the most prosperous period for windmills, and by 1862 there were thirty-three operating in Herts. However, by 1899 the number had fallen to seven. The miller here in 1882 was Mr W.J. Waylett. The windmill operated until 1895.

Section Eight

NAVIGATION

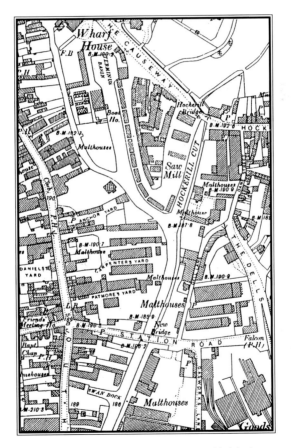

Opened in 1769, the waterway was instrumental in bringing prosperity to Bishop's Stortford. The town became a major supplier of malt to the brewers in London. It now has an atmosphere of quietness and serenity for the holiday-boat owners to enjoy.

Anno Sexto

Georgii III. Regis.

An Act for making and continuing navigable the River *Stort*, in the Counties of *Hertford* and *Essex*.

HEREAS by an Act passed in the Thirty-second Year of the Reign of His late Majesty King *George* the Second, intituled, *An Act for making the River* Stort *navigable, in the Counties of* Hertford *and* Essex, *from the* New Bridge *in the Town of* Bishop Stortford, *into the River* Lee, *near a Place called* The Rye, *in the County of* Hertford ; it is enacted, That the several Persons in the said Act named, shall be Commissioners for making the said River Stort navigable, and for putting the said Act in Execution,

Preamble reciting Act 32 Geo. II.

An extract from the amendment to an Act of George III of 1758–9 which allowed a change of directors of the River Stort Navigation.

To the Memory of
Sir GEORGE JACKSON Bar.[t]
afterwards
Sir GEORGE DUCKETT Bar.[t]
Judge Advocate of the Fleet.
who died 15th December 1822. Aged 97 Years.

He was for many Years a Secretary of the Admiralty
and a Member of Parliament for
Weymouth and Melcombe Regis and for Colchester

CAPTAIN COOK
of whom he was a zealous Friend and early Patron.
named after him
Point Jackson in New Zealand
and Port Jackson in New South Wales

In 1769
He made the River Stort navigable.
to this Town.

A portrait of Sir George Duckett and his memorial in St Michael's Church. Sir George died in 1822, aged ninety-seven, and is buried in the churchyard.

The Navigation of the STORT was made pursuant to an Act of Parliament of 6 GEO 3[d]. The Work was begun on 24 Sep[tr] 1766, and on 24 Oct 1769 two loaded Barges arrived in the Town of BISHOPS STORTFORD. The extent from the LEA to BISHOPS STORTFORD is 13 Miles 0 Furlongs

A stone plaque to commemorate the opening of the Stort Navigation. This was originally installed at Bishop's Stortford but is now in the British Waterways Board's Enfield Lock depot.

One of the few photographs of a sailing barge, at the head of the navigation, moored by the quay at Wharf House. The house was built by Sir George Duckett but was only occasionally used by him. It later became the offices of the Bishop's Stortford Urban District Council, until it was pulled down in 1973 to make way for the shopping precinct development.

The commemorative 1d token issued by Sir George Duckett in 1795 was struck at the Mint, Birmingham, for use on the waterway. On the obverse is a rebus of ducks and on the reverse is a general navigation scene.

A horse-drawn barge awaiting its load, *c.* 1880. The wharf is near the head of the navigation, and in the background are a crane and malthouse kiln tops.

South Mill Lock, *c.* 1905. Many of the locks in the upper part of the system were turf sided, as shown here.

The hand-operated crane at the head of the navigation, *c.* 1900.

An empty barge moored at Anchor Wharf. These vessels could carry 60 tons of cargo, and some were 70 ft long. The large rudder and tiller necessary to guide the horse-drawn and slow-moving barge are clearly shown.

Originally at South Mill Lock, this notice did not mean a casual ride on a canal barge, but a visit to the colonies.

On special occasions the boat could be used to give family and friends an outing on the water, followed by a picnic in a local farmer's field or on Wallbury Dells. This photograph dates from about 1900.

The navigation terminus basin, with warehouses on the left and the grounds of Wharf House to the right.

This postcard shows the malthouse, to the right, opposite the entrance to the terminus. In the distance is the crane which replaced the one shown on page 84.

Colonel Venn, Chairman of the Urban District Council, makes a speech to mark the celebrations to commemorate the 200th anniversary of the opening of the navigation in 1769.

At the head of the navigation, the crane (right) has been decorated and a goodly fleet of cruisers has filled the waterway to join the celebrations. Edwards Mill is in the background.

The more normal scene is shown in this view of a single visitor, *c.* 1960.

NOTICE TO MILLERS.   №.2

To *M⁻ Frogley*

Broxbourne MILL,

Broxbourne

LEE CONSERVANCY,

OFFICE :—12, FINSBURY CIRCUS,

LONDON, E.C.

SIR,

    I am directed by the Lee Conservancy Board to give you Notice that the Head Water of your Mill was ~~on the~~ *on the* ~~o'clock this~~ *1ᵒᵉ Aug* drawn down *18* inches below head by the working of the Mill, and to request that you will shut down and stop the Mill until the Water is raised to the proper height.

    And I have further to require you not to draw down the Water at any time, but to keep the same to the Statutory height, as required by the " River Lee Act," 45 Geo. III., cap. 69.

I am,

Yours obediently,

GEO : CORBLE,

Clerk.

~~Signature of Lockkeeper~~ *for Chas. N⁻ Tween*

Engineer

Lock.

Date *Aug. 2ⁿᵈ* 1906 *p 5 r.*

Time

The competition between the boat owners and the millers for sufficient water is indicated in this reminder issued in 1906. It instructs the millers not to let the water level fall too low.

STATION ROAD, GREAT EASTERN RAILWAY

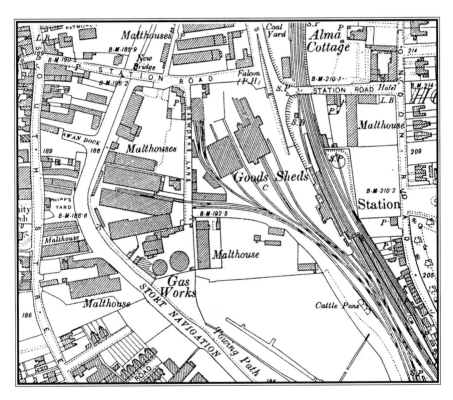

The North Eastern Counties Railway Company was one of the first to be established, and its line reached

Bishop's Stortford in 1842. The track was laid using a broad gauge system, which was soon replaced by the

present standard system. The line was taken over by the Great Eastern Railway Company in August 1862.

The railway was to have a great effect on the town's economy: both the coach and the waterway industries were

reduced virtually to extinction within sixty years. Now the railway in turn is under pressure to survive.

Station Road at the junction with South Street, *c.* 1900. Work and pleasure are side by side; a cart is going about its business, while the sparkling carriages approaching are taking part in the Whitsun parade. The gentleman on the left is Mr Davis (hairdresser), and the young lady opposite is Miss Edie Taylor, who stands in front of the Catherine Wheel public house.

The pace of life appears much slower here, *c.* 1890. This is probably New Bridge Street before it became Station Road. To the left is the entrance to Newman's Ferry, and visible in the distance are the tops of malthouse kilns, with their rotating caps.

The corner of Gasworks Lane (later Anchor Street, with The Hole in t' Wall, a Hawkes' public house, to the right, *c.* 1875. It is now the Rose and Crown.

The view north from Station Road bridge, *c.* 1910. A malthouse kiln is on the right, and the boys are walking past the wall and shed of the rope walk.

The view south from Station Road bridge, with Taylor's maltings on the immediate left and Anchor Wharf on the right. The chimneys on the skyline are those of Paradise Row, known locally as the 'Vatican', owing to the number of members of the Pope family living there.

Loading a wagon with 168 lb sacks of malt at H.A. & D. Taylor's. Station Road bridge is in the background.

The South Street bus depot, *c.* 1914. The National Bus Company staff pose with their fleet, which includes Tilley-Stevens solid-tyred buses. This is now the site of the East Herts District Council depot.

The Dells (now the Falcon). Situated opposite the railway station, the pub is still very successful, but it no longer has the adjacent good stabling and smithy which Alfred Reeve, the landlord, offered in 1890.

The railway reached Bishop's Stortford on 16 May 1842 and the original station is shown in this sketch. Depicted is a broad gauge locomotive, and its coaches, the design of which mimicked their predecessor, the stagecoach.

Bishop's Stortford railway station, *c.* 1870. In the forecourt are Mr Anstee and his staff. All linking transport was by horse and was to remain so for another thirty years.

Mr W.J. Anstee, stationmaster at Bishop's Stortford, *c.* 1870.

Three Great Eastern Railway type T26 locomotives in the sidings at Bishop's Stortford, *c.* 1901.

GREAT EASTERN RAILWAY.

Brewers' Exhibition at the Agricultural Hall

ON FRIDAY, OCTOBER 25th, 1895, CHEAP EXCURSION TICKETS will be issued to LONDON, as under:—

From	By Train at			Fare for the Double Journey
	a.m.	a.m.	a.m.	Third Class
Audley End	..	..	8 7	3s 6d
Newport	..	..	8 12	
Elsenham	..	..	8 21	
Stansted	..	..	8 26	
Bishop Stortford ..	..	8 16	..	3s 0d
Sawbridgeworth ..	7 20	..	..	
Harlow	7 25	..	..	2s 6d

Available for return from London (Liverpool-street) the same day, as under:—

At 7.32 or 9.20 p.m. to Harlow and Sawbridgeworth.
At 8.20 or 10.2 p.m. to Bishop Stortford.
At 8.20 p.m. to all other Stations.

WILLIAM BIRT,
General Manager.

London, Oct., 1895.

A Great Eastern Railway notice offering cheap excursion tickets to the Brewers' Exhibition in London, 1895.

Section Ten

MARKET SQUARE, KNIGHT STREET

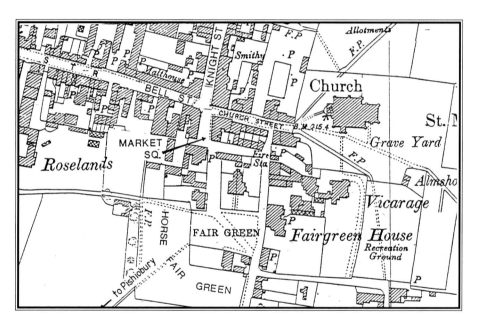

Fair Green, Market Square and Church Street enclose the medieval centre of Sawbridgeworth, and the town is very fortunate in keeping the features of its heritage so well defined. Fair Green still has a fair twice a year, on 22 April and 9 October. These have been held since 1447, when the charter was granted by King Henry VI to Sir John Leventhorpe.

Fair Green. Its medieval plan survives, but the green is no longer used for hiring fairs or for church ale-fairs.

Landlord Peter Taylor stands in front of the King William IV public house in Vantorts Road. Next to the pub is the Masonic Hall and then Fair Green House, one-time residence of Mr E.B. Barnard. In the distance is Corner House, home in 1970 to Sir John Newsom, author of the famous education report of 1963.

Market Square, as seen from Knight Street, with Lawrence's butcher's shop in the centre, 1900. The square was another fundamental village feature of the past. This square is smaller now, as a result of the encroachment of the buildings, and the market survives in name only. The Bell & Feathers hotel closed in 1910.

The Market House has had a long and varied history. It was built in about 1650 as a splendid residence, though the structure indicates that it has been used for trading. Later it was owned by Mr John Barnard, and used as offices to the malthouse at the rear. Subsequently it has been a nursing home, carpet warehouse and hotel.

Mr Albert Fish and his delivery van. It is also seen in the previous picture, outside Forrest Stores.

One of the last smithies in Sawbridgeworth, at 31a Knight Street, *c*. 1910. Standing outside are a helper (left), Mr Edward Hutley (centre) and Mr Alfred Taylor. For many years the building served as a wet-fish and fried-fish shop, run by the Smith family. It is now a Chinese fish and chip shop and restaurant.

Captain Ralph Allen produced a book on poultry egg production using Colman's Poultry Mustard, and there were so many orders for the publication that several carts were required to deliver them to the local post office.

Mr Sidney W. Parfect, headmaster of Fawbert & Barnard County Controlled School. He joined the school as a teacher in 1906 and retired in June 1938.

The school was ready to take advantage of the county call for more physical education in schools, and with the able help of Mr Kelsey the Fawbert & Barnard team had a run of victories in the 1911/12 and 1912/13 seasons.

LONDON ROAD, BELL STREET, CHURCH STREET

*Cock Street (now known as Bell Street) linked the village with the road to London and Cambridge. This
became the coaching road, via Knight Street and Mill Hill, to cross the river into Essex, on the way to
Chelmsford. Mine host at the Old Bell would no doubt have made them very welcome.*

Hoestock Road fire, 2 February 1905. At least six different postcard views of this fire were circulated.

Mr Truswell, the local photographer, must have been forewarned of the Aussies' progress through Sawbridgeworth, in order to be set up ready and waiting for the moment they passed his shop door. The picture dates from about 1915.

The junction of London Road and Bell Street, *c*. 1900. To the right is the shop of Mr J. Tarling, plumber and glazier. Clearly visible are the thatching, steep tiling and clapboard cladding with brick below, which are all typical of buildings in this region of East Anglia.

The same junction, but much changed, *c*. 1930. Mr W.H. Harris's baker's shop is on the corner (left). Opposite, the White Lion caters for a posse of the new-fangled motor cars.

At the outbreak of the First World War the King of Prussia was obliged to change its name to the King's Head. The pub stood near the turning for Bell Street. It closed in about 1970, to be replaced by the Kings Court flats.

S. Christy, butcher, at 5 Bell Street, *c.* 1920. The family trade had been in Bell Street since 1890.

Bell Street, *c.* 1980. The removal of the tree, near the malting hoist, caused several protests to be lodged, but progress prevailed.

John Fish, foreman of the road sweepers, stands with his long-handled broom and exchanges the latest news with his grandfather, Thomas Fish, on the corner of Bell Street and Market Square, *c.* 1914.

A horse fair in Bell Street with customers and vendors waiting for the auction to begin, April 1913. This picture shows the sack hoist (luccombe) on the left. It projects from the buildings which later became Star Supply Stores.

Firemen on display in Church Street, or have the horses not finished their breakfast? Much interest is shown on what must have been a school holiday, c. 1905. The gentleman in the doorway on the left is Mr Archer.

Turning out of Vantorts Road into Church Street, the 'steamer' returns from a fire, and presents an irresistible spectacle, c. 1905. The brick building behind is the old workhouse, which closed in 1835. The inmates moved to Bishop's Stortford.

Miss Norah Baker displays her dog outside the King William IV in Vantorts Road, *c.* 1935. Both the cottages on the left-hand side have been demolished for road widening. The first cottage was the home of Miss Becky Wood, and in the corner cottage lived the Howe family.

The Leicestershire Regiment pose outside the 'King Willie' with Peter Taylor jnr, the landlord. Billeted locally for a short time during the First World War, they were well liked, including the Army Heavyweight Boxing Champion, seated on the right.

NAVIGATION, MALTING

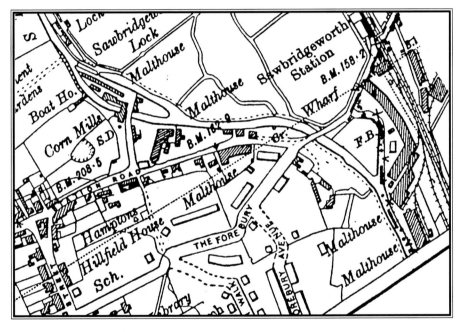

The industries of Sawbridgeworth were a scaled-down version of Bishop's Stortford's, and suffered a similar decline. Before the introduction of the railway, industrialists from London were choosing to move to the countryside, which helped to cushion the effects of decline. Robert Orchard (cocoa and tea dealer) was one who came to Sawbridgeworth, in about 1800.

The flourmill and maltings of Thomas Burton Ltd (Sawbridgeworth), 1955.

Unloading narrowboats by means of a grain elevator. Compared with humping quarter sacks or shovelling the load into quayside hoppers, this must have been the equivalent of a holiday cruise.

The millstream at Sawbridgeworth Mill maintained a flow sufficient to attract anglers with its promise of a good catch.

Mill House, the first house on the left, with a mansard roof. The re-use of materials is amply demonstrated by this house, which began life as a windmill on Harlow Common. When a road was built near the common in 1830, to accommodate the stagecoaches, the mill was sold and carried on a cart to Sawbridgeworth. The house has since been extended, but it retains some of the mill's frame, and the frame front faces the road.

Thomas Burton's Garrett steam lorries, *c.* 1925. Although the drivers had to ensure that there was a source of water available on their journeys, they were normally ready to compliment the engines on their smooth, quiet operation and their ability to climb any hill effortlessly. The lorries, with a fire underneath and a huge chain to drive the rear wheels, were a thing of wonder to children. Pictured from left to right: Mr David Howe, Mr W. Tant, Mr George Howe.

Standing at the garden gate are, from left to right, Mr Peter Brace, his Aunt Martha, Mrs Maria Brace and Mr Thomas Brace, *c.* 1880. Mr Brace snr was the manager of Burton's malthouse, nearby.

The Wharf, Station Road (formerly Mill Hill), *c.* 1880. In the background are Bridgefoot farmhouse and the malthouses, which both took advantage of the public wharf and crane when loading goods into the barges. The size of the barge can be appreciated when compared with the figures.

H.A. & D. Taylor's maltings. These were established in about 1886 from existing maltings. The malthouse complex produced a wide range of products, which included liquid and powder malt extracts – widely used by bakers, brewers, biscuit and toffee makers, chemists and others. The site closed in 1980 and is now occupied by flats, shops and light industry.

A winter scene at Sheering Mill on a chill and windless day, *c*. 1910. The exit tunnels of the millstream are clearly shown. The mill closed and was demolished in 1914.

Sheering Mill Lockhouse. Each lock-keeper had the length of the waterway above and below his lock to patrol. Mr Higgins (on the bridge) would cover as far as Tednambury Lock. The lock is turf-sided in this view.

This oil painting by Mr J.J. Perring depicts a horse-drawn barge as it is poled out of the lock. The horseman is coupling the towrope back on to the swingletree for the horse to take up the tow.

An aerial view of Sheering Mill Lock, 1948. The lock is brick-sided and only the millrace remains to indicate the position of the mill. Between the waterway and the railway is the factory of Walter Lawrence, where quality internal and external fittings for the building trade were made until it closed in 1985. The course of the River Stort is on the left of the navigation.

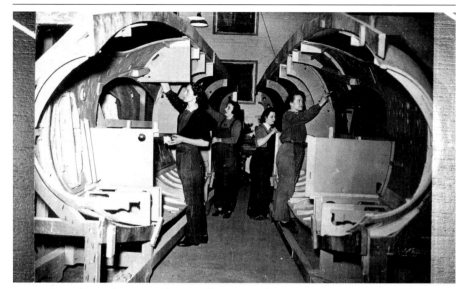

Lawrence's changed to aircraft manufacture in the Second World War, and here the ladies are coating the inside of a de Havilland Mosquito fuselage.

The 1,000th 'Mossie' fuselage is despatched to the Hatfield factory for finishing. Portraits of President Roosevelt, Prime Minister Churchill and Comrade Stalin have been added for the benefit of the photographer.

Mr Edmund Broughton Barnard celebrated the opening of the YMCA Soldiers' Social Centre at Shaftesbury Hall, on the site of the present United Services Club, with a garden party in the grounds of Fair Green Lodge in July 1915.

Edmund Broughton Barnard OBE, DL. He was a JP, MP for Kidderminster and Chairman of Hertfordshire County Council.

The funeral of Sir E.B. Barnard, who died on 27 January 1930, aged seventy-three. It was a notable occasion. The entrance to the church was lined with constables, and Mr H. Knight, Chief Constable of Hertfordshire (seen here to the left of the undertakers), led the cortège. The numerous mourners included the Lord Lieutenant of Hertfordshire (Viscount Hampden), the High Sheriff (Captain E. Martin-Smith) and the Earl of Clarenden.

As one moved about among the crowd of on-lookers after the funeral, one heard on all sides expressions of deep regret, expressions that obviously came from the heart. One old woman of the poorer class was overheard to remark. " Aye, God bless him ! ' Teddy' Barnard was one of the best : he'll be missed and wanted, by many a poor soul that he has been good to ! " Another remark overheard was, " He was always ready to give a bit of help to them what needed it ! "

Though not exactly grammatical, that seems a fitting epitaph to a great and generous soul.

Immediately before the funeral a short service, conducted by the Rev. A. J. Gillson, was held at the house, for the ladies of the household who were unable to attend the service at the Church and graveside. Among these was Miss Ellen Rochester, the housekeeper, who has been in the service of Sir Edmund Barnard and his family for about 70 years.

An extract from the obituary of Sir E.B. Barnard in the *Herts and Essex Observer* of 1 February 1930.

'Nellie' Emma Brace, *c.* 1906. This is a delightful picture of a young girl carefully posed in the photographer's studio; she is holding her favourite doll and has one hand on the balustrade to steady herself during the exposure.

The local lads pose on their rigid frame motor cycle, *c.* 1935. Left to right: Fred Puncher, Les Brown, Harold Vale, Richard Chadwick. Richard says they rode down the farm road in this way and it was very uncomfortable.

A grand display by the Volunteer Fire Brigade on Fair Green, *c.* 1910. Mounted, from left to right: E. Millar, W. Lacey, H. Taylor, H. Boatman, W. Stacey, A.J. Archer, ? White, J. Searle. Standing: W.G. Prior, W. Collins, A. Nockolds, R.A. Parmiter, W. Morris, H. Traveller, Dr Collins, Captain Allen. Seated: H. Baker, ? Ginn. W. Collins was only ten years old, the youngest fireman in the country.

A later version of a similar display, *c.* 1938. Top, from left to right: W. Searle, J. Searle, B. Taylor, J. Webb, -?-. Middle: W. White, J. Baker, F. Wright, J. Taylor, J. Riches, -?-, -?-, L. Clements. Standing: H. Taylor, Dr Hailey (Captain), W. Prior.

The Sawbridgeworth 'Optimists', presenting the *Street Singer* at the Assembly Hall, 1935. The principals are D. Pavely and Jean Atkinson.

The Assembly Hall, on the corner of Bullfields and Station Road, *c.* 1911. Concerts by local groups were held here, and during the Second World War the local airmen put on a concert for everybody's enjoyment. The hall was demolished in about 1970.

Sawbridgeworth railway station, looking towards the Down line to Cambridge, *c*. 1910. Here the station has gas lighting and a wooden signal-box; the crossing gates were opened from inside the signal-box by a hand wheel.

A Great Eastern Railway steam train type Y10 passes through on the Up line to Liverpool Street, *c*. 1920. The stationmaster's ample house is in the background. The gates on the left lead to the yard of the Railway Inn.

High Wych Windmill. This must have been a prominent feature on the skyline of Sawbridgeworth village. It was built in 1824 and was worked by Tim Puckle in 1841, James Dorkins from 1850 to 1855, John Stewart & Son from 1872 to 1874, and James Ward in 1875. The mill was dismantled and moved to Little Dunmow. Some remains of it are still visible.

High Wych village green. It is still a very rural looking green. It retains its two public houses, the Rising Sun and the Half Moon, but the village pump, with its large hand wheel, has now been removed.

HERE LYETH BVRIED EDWARD LEVENTHORP ESQVIRE WHO DIED IN DECEMB
155¹⁴ BEING ẙ ELDEST SONNE OF THOMAS LEVENTHORP ESQVIRE & ELIZA⁴
BETH HIS WIFE ẙ DAVGHTER OF • BARLEE OF ALDBVRY ESQVIRE.
THEIRE ELDEST SONE WAS ALSO EDWARD WHO MARRIED MARY PARKER THE SE⁹
COND DAVGHTER OF Sᵗ HARRY PARKER KNIGHT ẙ ELDEST SONE OF HARRY LO MOᴿ

Scale ⌐_____⌐ 1 Feet

Edward Leventhorp, Esq., 1551, and wife Elizabeth.
ENGRAVED C. 1600.

Edward Leventhorpe Esq. and his wife Elizabeth, 1600. The Leventhorpe family and Shingle Hall, Sawbridgeworth, were associated from 1410 until 1679. Edward was the grandfather of the first baronet, Sir John Leventhorpe. This brass shows in great detail the dress of the period, and was possibly engraved by Gerard Johnson of Southwark (1541–1612).

Acknowledgements

I am most grateful to the Hertfordshire Record Office and the Bishop's Stortford and District Local History Society for permission to use the photographs in this book. I would also like to acknowledge the use of the following:

W.E.A. Story of Sawbridgeworth, *Prehistory to the Present*
—— *Churches and the People*
—— *Century of Village Schooling*
Bishop's Stortford & District Local History Society, *Bishop's Stortford – a Short History*
J.G. Smith, *Bishop's Stortford Hostelries*
V. Sparrow, *Yesterday's Stortford*
The notes of the late Mr and Mrs K.E. Wilson
Map details of Bishop's Stortford from the Ordnance Survey sheet of Essex, XXII.15, 2nd edn, 1897
Map details of Sawbridgeworth from the Ordnance Survey sheets of Herts, XXII.6, 10, 2nd edn, 1897 and XXXI.5, 2nd edn, 1898

I am greatly indebted to all the staff at the Bishop's Stortford Local History Museum for all their assistance with information, and particularly to my wife Doreen.

BRITAIN IN OLD PHOTOGRAPHS

To order any of these titles please telephone Littlehampton Book Services on 01903 721596

ALDERNEY

Alderney: A Second Selection, *B Bonnard*

BEDFORDSHIRE

Bedfordshire at Work, *N Lutt*

BERKSHIRE

Maidenhead, *M Hayles & D Hedges*
Around Maidenhead, *M Hayles & B Hedges*
Reading, *P Southerton*
Reading: A Second Selection, *P Southerton*
Sandhurst and Crowthorne, *K Dancy*
Around Slough, *J Hunter & K Hunter*
Around Thatcham, *P Allen*
Around Windsor, *B Hedges*

BUCKINGHAMSHIRE

Buckingham and District, *R Cook*
High Wycombe, *R Goodearl*
Around Stony Stratford, *A Lambert*

CHESHIRE

Cheshire Railways, *M Hitches*
Chester, *S Nichols*

CLWYD

Clwyd Railways, *M Hitches*

CLYDESDALE

Clydesdale, *Lesmahagow Parish Historical Association*

CORNWALL

Cornish Coast, *T Bowden*
Falmouth, *P Gilson*
Lower Fal, *P Gilson*
Around Padstow, *M McCarthy*
Around Penzance, *J Holmes*
Penzance and Newlyn, *J Holmes*
Around Truro, *A Lyne*
Upper Fal, *P Gilson*

CUMBERLAND

Cockermouth and District, *J Bernard Bradbury*
Keswick and the Central Lakes, *J Marsh*
Around Penrith, *F Boyd*
Around Whitehaven, *H Fancy*

DERBYSHIRE

Derby, *D Buxton*
Around Matlock, *D Barton*

DEVON

Colyton and Seaton, *T Gosling*
Dawlish and Teignmouth, *G Gosling*
Devon Aerodromes, *K Saunders*
Exeter, *P Thomas*
Exmouth and Budleigh Salterton, *T Gosling*
From Haldon to Mid-Dartmoor, *T Hall*
Honiton and the Otter Valley, *J Yallop*
Around Kingsbridge, *K Tanner*
Around Seaton and Sidmouth, *T Gosling*
Seaton, Axminster and Lyme Regis, *T Gosling*

DORSET

Around Blandford Forum, *B Cox*
Bournemouth, *M Colman*
Bridport and the Bride Valley, *J Burrell & S Humphries*
Dorchester, *T Gosling*
Around Gillingham, *P Crocker*

DURHAM

Darlington, *G Flynn*
Darlington: A Second Selection, *G Flynn*
Durham People, *M Richardson*
Houghton-le-Spring and Hetton-le-Hole, *K Richardson*
Houghton-le-Spring and Hetton-le-Hole:
    A Second Selection, *K Richardson*
Sunderland, *S Miller & B Bell*
Teesdale, *D Coggins*
Teesdale: A Second Selection, *P Raine*
Weardale, *J Crosby*
Weardale: A Second Selection, *J Crosby*

DYFED

Aberystwyth and North Ceredigion,
    Dyfed Cultural Services Dept
Haverfordwest, *Dyfed Cultural Services Dept*
Upper Tywi Valley, *Dyfed Cultural Services Dept*

ESSEX

Around Grays, *B Evans*

GLOUCESTERSHIRE

Along the Avon from Stratford to Tewkesbury, *J Jeremiah*
Cheltenham: A Second Selection, *R Whiting*
Cheltenham at War, *P Gill*
Cirencester, *J Welsford*
Around Cirencester, *E Cuss & P Griffiths*
Forest, The, *D Mullin*
Gloucester, *J Voyce*
Around Gloucester, *A Sutton*
Gloucester: From the Walwin Collection, *J Voyce*
North Cotswolds, *D Viner*
Severn Vale, *A Sutton*
Stonehouse to Painswick, *A Sutton*
Stroud and the Five Valleys, *S Gardiner & L Padin*
Stroud and the Five Valleys: A Second Selection,
    S Gardiner & L Padin
Stroud's Golden Valley, *S Gardiner & L Padin*
Stroudwater and Thames & Severn Canals,
    E Cuss & S Gardiner
Stroudwater and Thames & Severn Canals: A Second
    Selection, *E Cuss & S Gardiner*
Tewkesbury and the Vale of Gloucester, *C Hilton*
Thornbury to Berkeley, *J Hudson*
Uley, Dursley and Cam, *A Sutton*
Wotton-under-Edge to Chipping Sodbury, *A Sutton*

GWYNEDD

Anglesey, *M Hitches*
Gwynedd Railways, *M Hitches*
Around Llandudno, *M Hitches*
Vale of Conwy, *M Hitches*

HAMPSHIRE

Gosport, *J Sadden*
Portsmouth, *P Rogers & D Francis*

HEREFORDSHIRE

Herefordshire, *A Sandford*

HERTFORDSHIRE

Barnet, *I Norrie*
Hitchin, *A Fleck*
St Albans, *S Mullins*
Stevenage, *M Appleton*

ISLE OF MAN

The Tourist Trophy, *B Snelling*

ISLE OF WIGHT

Newport, *D Parr*
Around Ryde, *D Parr*

JERSEY

Jersey: A Third Selection, *R Lemprière*

KENT

Bexley, *M Scott*
Broadstairs and St Peter's, *J Whyman*
Bromley, Keston and Hayes, *M Scott*
Canterbury: A Second Selection, *D Butler*
Chatham and Gillingham, *P MacDougall*
Chatham Dockyard, *P MacDougall*
Deal, *J Broady*
Early Broadstairs and St Peter's, *B Wootton*
East Kent at War, *D Collyer*
Eltham, *J Kennett*
Folkestone: A Second Selection, *A Taylor & E Rooney*
Goudhurst to Tenterden, *A Guilmant*
Gravesend, *R Hiscock*
Around Gravesham, *R Hiscock & D Grierson*
Herne Bay, *J Hawkins*
Lympne Airport, *D Collyer*
Maidstone, *I Hales*
Margate, *R Clements*
RAF Hawkinge, *R Humphreys*
RAF Manston, *RAF Manston History Club*
RAF Manston: A Second Selection,
    RAF Manston History Club
Ramsgate and Thanet Life, *D Perkins*
Romney Marsh, *E Carpenter*
Sandwich, *C Wanostrocht*
Around Tonbridge, *C Bell*
Tunbridge Wells, *M Rowlands & I Beavis*
Tunbridge Wells: A Second Selection,
    M Rowlands & I Beavis
Around Whitstable, *C Court*
Wingham, Adisham and Littlebourne, *M Crane*

LANCASHIRE

Around Barrow-in-Furness, *J Garbutt & J Marsh*
Blackpool, *C Rothwell*
Bury, *J Hudson*
Chorley and District, *J Smith*
Fleetwood, *C Rothwell*
Heywood, *J Hudson*
Around Kirkham, *C Rothwell*
Lancashire North of the Sands, *J Garbutt & J Marsh*
Around Lancaster, *S Ashworth*
Lytham St Anne's, *C Rothwell*
North Fylde, *C Rothwell*
Radcliffe, *J Hudson*
Rossendale, *B Moore & N Dunnachie*

LEICESTERSHIRE

Around Ashby-de-la-Zouch, *K Hillier*
Charnwood Forest, *I Keil, W Humphrey & D Wix*
Leicester, *D Burton*
Leicester: A Second Selection, *D Burton*
Melton Mowbray, *T Hickman*
Around Melton Mowbray, *T Hickman*
River Soar, *D Wix, P Shacklock & I Keil*
Rutland, *T Clough*
Vale of Belvoir, *T Hickman*
Around the Welland Valley, *S Mastoris*

LINCOLNSHIRE

Grimsby, *J Tierney*
Around Grimsby, *J Tierney*
Grimsby Docks, *J Tierney*
Lincoln, *D Cuppleditch*